INVEST LIKE A ZEN MASTER AND LIVE HAPPILY EVER AFTER

INVEST LIKE A ZEN MASTER AND LIVE HAPPILY EVER AFTER

Helen Raleigh, CFA

Copyright © 2015, Helen Raleigh. All rights reserved. Unauthorized use and/or duplication of this material without express and written permission from the author and/or owner is strictly prohibited.

Contents

Preface 1

Chapter 1: What Does the Elephant Look Like? 5

Chapter 2: The Temptation 11

Chapter 3: Who is Zuikan? 19

Chapter 4: Maybe 25

Chapter 5: It's All About Perspective 33

Chapter 6: Cliffhanger 39

Chapter 7: The Fake Monk 47

Chapter 8: Can You Make an Egg Stand? 55

Conclusion: How Long Does it Take to Become a Master? ... 61

References 63

About the Author 67

Preface

At first glance, you may think the title of this book seems illogical. Zen is a school of Buddhism that originated in China during the 6th century. How could Zen have anything to do with 21st century Investing? Well, let me tell you a famous Zen story. It is called a *Cup of Tea*.

> *Nan-in, a Japanese master during the Meiji era (1868-1912), received a university professor who came to inquire about Zen.*
>
> *Nan-in served tea. He poured his visitor's cup full, and then kept on pouring.*
>
> *The professor watched the overflow until he no longer could restrain himself. "It is overfull. No more will go in!"*
>
> *"Like this cup," Nan-in said, "you are full of your own opinions and speculations. How can I show you Zen unless you first empty your cup?"*

Just like Master Nan-in, I cannot tell you how to invest like a Zen master unless you first clear your mind and get rid of your preconceived notions of what investing is or isn't. This book is not about investment strategies, and it certainly doesn't contain any hot stock tips. Instead, this book advocates changing your behaviors as an investor. There probably isn't a message in this book that most people don't already know, or haven't heard at least once. Yet, during my 15-year career in the financial services industry, I've witnessed investors, many of whom are intelligent and successful in their respective professional fields, repeatedly commit the same types of mistakes.

Do you believe as an investor you can achieve happiness, financial security, and inner peace at the same time? The truth is that the only barrier standing between you and your ultimate wealth and happiness is *you*, or more accurately, your own behaviors. You cannot control the stock market; you cannot control the economy; you cannot control your spouse, or your teenaged kids; many don't have much control of the type of work they do and how much money they make. The only thing each one of us has 100% control of is our own behavior. As financial adviser and author Nick Murray points out, "The single most important variable in the quest for equity investment success is also the only variable you ultimately control: your own behavior."

Throughout this book, I want to point out poor behaviors you should avoid as well as good behaviors you should have but are doing infrequently, or not at all. Good behaviors not only make you a better investor, but also a happier person. But this book is not a boring lecture or scolding. Each chapter except the last begins with an interesting story from the teaching of Zen. The Zen stories I've included in the book have had great influence on my own behavior and philosophy. One thing to know about Zen is that Zen masters pass on their wisdom through stories. These metaphorical stories are generally short but insightful. They focus less on giving us moral lessons about right and wrong, and more on enlightening us to discover the truth on our own. It is common that every person can learn different things from the same Zen story because we are all different people with different experiences. I am writing this book to share with you my learning. It is OK if you learn something different from these stories. Even if our conclusions differ, hopefully the wisdom gained from these stories will lead you to a better state of mind not just as an investor, but as a human being, which will in turn bring you inner peace and long-lasting happiness.

Chapter 1
What Does the Elephant Look Like?

Several citizens ran into a hot argument about God and different religions, and each one could not agree on a common answer. So they came to the Lord Buddha to find out what exactly God looks like.

The Buddha asked his disciples to get a large, magnificent elephant and four blind men. He then brought the four blind men to the elephant and told them to find out what the elephant "looked" like.

The first blind man touched the elephant's leg and reported that it "looked" like a pillar. The second blind man touched the elephant's tummy and said that an elephant was a wall. The third blind man touched the elephant's ear and said that it was a piece of cloth. The fourth blind man hold on to the tail and described the elephant as a piece of rope. And all of them ran into a hot argument about the "appearance" of an elephant and all of them insisted he was right.

The Buddha asked the citizens: "Each blind man had touched the elephant but each of them gives a different description of the animal. Which answer is right?"

The blind men drew their conclusion of what an elephant looks like through the senses they trusted and relied on—touching and feeling. There is nothing wrong with this approach in the beginning. When we explore the unknown, it is natural to make judgments based on our past experiences and rely on the tools and skills we're used to depending on. However, the blind men's overconfidence in their senses made no room in their mind for what they couldn't touch and feel. Consequently, they were obsessed with one small section of truth and lost the "big picture."

It is important to have confidence in your decision. People gain confidence through experience and knowledge. In author Earl Gray Stevens's words, "Confidence, like art, never comes from having all the answers; it comes from being open to all the questions." But overconfidence often leads to misguided belief, which in turn prevents us from giving the benefit of the doubt to different ideas and beliefs.

As humans, we are wired to be overconfident. We tend to overestimate our looks, wealth, and luck, and we underestimate risks. One of the best known examples is from Ola Svenson's (1981) finding that 93% of American drivers rate themselves as better than the median. Prior to the 2008 housing market bust, many of us heard at least once from someone we knew who bragged about their success in the real estate market. Very few were willing to share how much losses they had to endure in the following years.

Professor Hersh Shefrin wrote in 1999 that "There are two main implications of investor overconfidence. The first is that investors take bad bets because they fail to realize that they are at an informational disadvantage. The second is that they trade more frequently than is prudent, which leads to excessive trading volume." A study released in 2014 by DALBAR, a financial services market research firm, offers empirical evidence of Shefrin's point. The study found that from 1984 to 2013, the Standard & Poor's 500 index had annual gains around 11.11% , while the average investor earned just 3.69%. In other words, average investors' returns lagged behind market-index returns almost 8% on an annual basis. Yet many investors still believe they can find that "secret sauce" to make them instantly wealthy. DALBAR's study concluded that "No matter what the state of the mutual fund industry, boom or bust: Investment results are more dependent on investor behavior than on fund performance."

Nothing breeds mistakes more than a past success-induced overconfidence. In a bull market, everyone becomes an investment genius. But even investment professionals cannot avoid mental hiccups. A recent example of overconfidence is JP Morgan's CEO Jamie Dimon. Under his leadership, JP Morgan survived the 2008 economic crisis relatively unscathed. Dimon often bragged that JP Morgan had a "fortress balance sheet." Yet in April and May of 2012, a JP Morgan trader in London, nicknamed "London Whale," incurred $6.2 billion in trading losses. When those trades were first reported by the *Wall Street Journal*, Dimon famously dismissed the report as a "tempest in a teapot." His past success certainly blinded his judgment. No wonder Mark Twain noted, "It ain't what you don't know that gets you into trouble. It's what you know for sure that just ain't so."

So how can you overcome a tendency toward overconfidence?

First, strike a balance between confidence and humility. The first test of a truly great man is his humility. By humility I don't mean constantly casting doubts about yourself. Practicing humility when making investment decisions means gaining a clear understanding of the source of your confidence and its limitations. We need humility to keep ourselves on a balanced footing. In his book *Thinking Fast and Slow*, Daniel Kahneman suggested asking yourself the following questions when you feel confident about your investment decision:

- Where does my confidence come from?
- How good is my story? Not as a story, but how good is my story in the sense of how much evidence supports it?

Only people who feel insecure about themselves have the need to constantly promote their worth to other people. My mother always warned me that when a person starts thinking that he is invincible; he is actually not too far away from failure. Confidence and humility are two sides of the same coin.

Second, don't presume to know all the answers. Taoism identified four phrases of learning:

- You don't know what you don't know.
- You know what you don't know.
- You know what you know.
- You don't know what you know.

The conclusion of this learning process is that the more you know, the less you know. Just like economist and columnist Thomas Sowell observed, "It takes considerable knowledge just to realize the extent of your own ignorance." Since you don't have all the answers, make learning a lifelong habit. Wise investors always set aside time for reading and thinking.

Many people want to know the secret of Warren Buffett's investment success. In the most recent letter to shareholders, Buffett's long-time friend and partner, Charles Munger, observed (of Buffett), "His first priority would be reservation of much time for quiet reading and thinking, particularly that which might advance his determined learning, no matter how old he became." We all can learn from Buffett and become a lifetime student.

Third, be ready to acknowledge you can be wrong. Expecting you can be wrong will help you let go of your overgrown ego and open you up to different ideas and opinions. Excessive confidence is harmful, while a diversity of ideas is something we should encourage. Even when facts vindicate you, be thankful that different opinions exist. Otherwise, as British philosopher John Stuart Mill famously said, "If the opinion is right, they are deprived of the opportunity of exchanging error for truth; if wrong, they lose, what is almost as great a benefit, the clearer perception and livelier impression of truth, produced by its collision with error."

Only a confident yet humble person can recognize his own limitations. You will be a great investor if you can balance your confidence with humility. Remember, "We come nearest to the great when we are great in humility." (Rabindranath Tagore)

謙虛

Chinese for "Humility"

Chapter 2

The Temptation

Two monks were returning to the monastery in the evening. It had rained and there were puddles of water on the roadsides. At one place a beautiful young woman was standing, unable to walk across because of a puddle of water. The elder of the two monks went up to her, lifted her up, carried her over the puddle of water, left her on the other side of the road, and continued his way to the monastery.

The young monk was shocked by the elder monk's behavior, because one of the vows that monks have to take is not to touch any women. In the evening the younger monk came to the elder monk and said, "Master, is it true that as monks we shouldn't touch a woman?"

The elder monk answered "Yes."

Then the younger monk asks again, "But then Master, did you break the vow when you lifted that woman on the roadside?"

The elder monk smiled at him and told him, "I left her on the other side of the road, but you are still carrying her."

This is a story about how to deal with temptation. Every time I read the last line, I can't help but smile and try to imagine the puzzled look of the poor young monk. He must have studied the Buddha's teachings very hard, word for word. Yet those words were not sufficient to help him fight off the thoughts of the beautiful young lady. No wonder he was so shocked by his master's behavior, which left him so confused.

Life is full of temptations. Investing, in particular, can be a tempting activity. The flashing numbers on the screen and the colored arrows constantly stimulate investors' brains. In addition, media organizations know how to entice investors with 24-hour coverage, hot tips, and catchy headlines such as "Three stocks are ready to take off" or "Five moves smart investors are making right now."

Unfortunately, many ordinary investors easily fall for such temptations. They typically let their emotions dictate their investment decisions by reacting to all the various tips and events and making hasty trades without studying them. The temptation to make a big killing in the stock market is so strong that many retail investors become sensation seekers who constantly search for the next piece of information that can make them rich overnight, and their adrenaline levels rise when the stock market is in action. In a way, these investors are gambling their money in the market, rather than actually investing their money. In fact, in a study of a group of 12 people who played a game in which they could win or lose money, the subjects' brain scan images were nearly identical to those of cocaine addicts (Sehgal, 2015).

Like a herd of sheep, many investors chase returns by jumping on board after a particular stock or a particular index had a streak of reaching new highs, or cashing out their positions after things have gone bad. Consequently, these investors often end up being several steps behind the market movement and have nothing to show for their actions except poor investment returns. When we let temptation lead us, we open ourselves to regret: regret of missing the gains and regret of not selling soon enough.

So what can we do to fight off temptations?

Step one: Set physical distance between you and the temptation. The natural defensive reaction is to barricade yourself from temptation: don't look, don't touch, pretend it is not there. Have you ever watched the marshmallow test video? The marshmallow test was developed by the legendary psychologist Walter Mischel in the late 1960s. In this experiment, young children between the ages of 4 and 6 were given a choice between having one marshmallow now or two marshmallows later if they waited 15 minutes. Some kids couldn't resist the temptation at all and ate the marshmallow right away, but most would engage in efforts to fight off temptation, such as covering their eyes, shifting their gaze from the marshmallow, or banging their heads against the table. In short, they tried all sorts of activities to distract themselves from the temptation, and many succeeded.

Setting physical distance or boundaries between oneself and the temptation is an effective way of self-control because of how our brain works. In his book *The Marshmallow Test,* Mischel explains how the prefrontal cortex of our brain can either activate a hot system to "deal with immediate rewards and threats," or activate a cool system to "deal with delayed consequences." So if you as an investor tend to chase hot stock tips, one of the many things you can do is to stay away from the 24-hour financial news cycle from time to time. That is what money manager Guy Spier did. In a *Wall Street Journal* article, Spier described that after he realized how flawed the brain can be, he set up a practical workaround to escape temptation and bad ideas. For example, worried that knowing the prices of his holdings would make him want to trade, he checks their market value only once a week, and he often turns off his firm's data terminal. Have these tactics helped? It is hard to quantify, but he has beaten the S&P 500 by 5.5 points annually since 2008.

For many investors, however, merely setting up the physical distance is not enough. The notion that you cannot have it makes the temptation that much more irresistible. Have you ever played the game that asks you not to think about something, like a white elephant, yet it turns out that is all you can think about? Just like the young monk or those who have played this game, many investors cannot stop thinking about the possibility that they may miss a huge run up in the market. Therefore, in addition to putting some physical distance between you and the temptations to trade, many investors could benefit from following step two.

Step two: Establish a decision parameter and stick to it religiously. For example, you can establish a sell parameter before you start investing. Let's say you know that you will lose sleep if the value of your investment drops more than 5%. You can set -5% as your sell trigger. By doing so, you know when to exit the market and minimize your loss. You can also set a sell trigger in the upper end. Since no investment will go up in a straight line forever, it is important to know when to recognize your gain. For example, you can set a sell trigger if the value of your investment rises above 20%. This kind of discipline is especially important in a bull market. If you become greedy and ride a winning investment for too long, you may end up losing the value of your investment because the stock market can move in an opposite direction very quickly.

Similarly, you can set parameters of when to buy a particular investment. If you are not an active trader, you can use your annual portfolio rebalancing to achieve a similar result. When you first set up your portfolio, you or your investment adviser will decide the percentage of the fund that will be invested in stocks (or stock funds) and how much will go to bonds (or bond funds). This original asset allocation in terms of percentage of stocks versus bonds can serve as your decision parameter.

For example, let's say an investor wants a 60-40 split between stocks and bonds. During the year, the market has had a nice and strong run, which results in the asset allocation being 65% in stocks and 35% in bonds. Rebalancing your portfolio back to its original 60-40 stock versus bond split on an annual basis will force you to sell some winning assets and buy some losing assets in order to get your portfolio back to the original asset allocation.

You can choose your decision parameters in different ways and frequencies. But in order for these decision parameters to be successful, you have to follow them religiously. If you constantly override them, they are useless in preventing you from making mistakes that cost you money. A study done by Barclays concluded that "emotional trading can cost an investor about 20% in returns over the 10-year period studied. Investors who prevented themselves from over-trading through specific strategies were, on average, 12% wealthier than those who did not use self-control mechanisms." (Ayres, et. al, 2011)

Being disciplined with your investment decisions and trading activities probably won't guarantee that you will beat the market in terms of investment return. But you can rest assured that you will earn a good return in the long run by avoiding costly behavior-driven mistakes.

Step three: resist temptation by having a clear vision of future benefits. I was born and raised in China. Growing up, I remember no matter how difficult life was, my parents somehow managed to find fish for our New Year's Eve "feast" every year. At the center of our dinner table on New Year's Eve, there sat the fish with its head and tail intact. We were told not to touch it and just look at it. It was meant to be saved for consumption on New Year's Day. For us little kids, it was a cruel punishment that we were not allowed to touch the fish when the aroma from it was so irresistible. But my parents always said that saving the fish dish for the next year was important. It meant we would not go hungry next year because the Chinese word for *fish* "鱼," sounds similar to another Chinese word "余," which means *extra*. By saving the fish dish, we learned not to consume all we had at once and always remembered to save something extra for the future.

Saving the fish dish was the first personal finance lesson that my parents taught me, and they reinforced this valuable lesson year after year through the fish dish on New Year's Eve. This lesson has served me well. When I came to the

U.S. 18 years ago, I had less than $100 in my pocket. I not only worked hard, but I also learned to always save a little extra for future. Now, I am the founder of Red Meadow Advisors LLC, a company that focuses on helping others achieve financial freedom.

I feel deep gratitude that I am living in the richest and most powerful nation in the world. At the same time, I am concerned by how many people are trapped by debt. According to a report by Bloomberg, consumer debt in America has reached an all-time high of $3.2 trillion. The same report also reminds us "that consumption, financed by debt, is not the path to resilient growth." The road to prosperity is simpler than many people think. It begins with living within your means, delaying gratification and always saving some extra for the future. We do not have to keep up with the Joneses.

As author Simon Sinek said, "The big picture doesn't just come from distance; it also comes from time." Temptations come and go; however, as long as you stick to a disciplined approach, knowing what is right for you, knowing what your future reward will be, all you have to do is to acknowledge temptation's existence and let them pass. Do not let temptations alter your own path toward prosperity. Don't eat your marshmallow now.

自律

Chinese for "self-control"

Chapter 3
Who is Zuikan?

Zuikan was a Zen master who always used to address himself. "Zuikan?" he would call. And then he would answer. "Yes!" "Zuikan?" "Yes!" Of course he was living all alone in his small hut, and of course he knew who he was, but sometimes he lost himself. And whenever he lost himself, he would address himself, "Zuikan?" "Yes!"

Master Zuikan calls himself out as his way of practicing how not to lose himself—be true to himself. Aristotle said that "knowing yourself is the beginning of all wisdom." The biggest mistake a person can make is to lose himself in the process of pursuing something, whether for wealth, status, or relationship. Zen is all about discovering your inner self, being true to yourself.

Yes, no one is perfect. Each one of us should be keenly aware of our own limitations, flaws, and imperfections. That is the humility we talk about in Chapter 1. "I don't know" are three simple words that most people are terrified to say. Research has shown that most humans think they're smarter, more talented, and generally above average in comparison to everyone else. This is called *optimal bias*. When you don't think you are smarter than everyone else, and instead are honest about what you don't know, your flaws and weaknesses, you are already ahead of the game.

A smart investor, first and foremost, admits things he or she doesn't know. No one can predict whether tomorrow the Dow Jones Industrial Average Index will go up or down, or by how much. Most talking heads on CNBC or Bloomberg give wrong predictions on the economy. Arrogance will cost you a lot of money. Only when you acknowledge there are things you don't know, you can decide whether to invest in only things you know, like Warren Buffett does, or outsource your investments to professionals.

Knowing yourself also means to expect and be prepared to make mistakes. To put this into perspective, you need to realize that professionals make mistakes too. Michael Jordan, arguably the greatest basketball player of all time, declared: "I've missed more than 9,000 shots in my career. I've lost almost 300 games. Twenty-six times, I've been trusted to take the game-winning shot and missed. I've failed over and over and over again in my life. And that is why I succeed." Recognizing flaws and imperfections can motivate us to get better. Intel founder Andy Grove said in an interview that "You must understand your mistakes. Study the hell out of them. You're not going to have the chance of making the same mistake again—you can't step into the river again at the same place and the same time—but you will have the chance of making a similar mistake."

Some investors hold on to an investment far too long for emotional reasons; maybe he inherited some shares from someone with whom he had a strong emotional bond. Some investors are just too prideful to admit they made mistakes, but the best investors never tie their ego to their trades. They own their mistakes and are willing to cut their losses and move on. So don't be married to your investments until it is too late to sell.

For investors, knowing yourself also means asking yourself what kind of investor you are. Are you a Warren Buffett type of buy-and-hold investor, or you are an active trader like those guys and gals on CNBC's "Fast Money"? Don't choose a style just because it is popular or because it works for someone else. One of the typical behaviors investors exhibit is a psychological disorder called "I'm-Missing-it." It develops when people believe that they are missing their chance to make more money on their investments. The condition is exacerbated by the amount of money they hear somebody else is making.

Choose a style based on what you are comfortable with. If you don't have any deep conviction on any particular investment or you don't find following market movements exciting, you probably are not an active investor. So a good option for you is to invest in index funds that track the performance of the broad market. Even if you are an active investor and find tracking market movements on a daily basis is exciting, I don't recommend putting all your financial net eggs in one basket. Think long and hard before you invest in any single stock. Ask yourself, if all these investments lost half their values or even evaporate tomorrow, will you still be able to sleep at night or will you still be able to meet your financial goal?

No matter what kind of investor you are, don't forget the importance of sticking to a preset decision parameter when you invest. As we mentioned before, the decision parameter can be either your target asset allocation mix or rules on when to enter or exit a market. It is much easier to be disciplined about following your decision parameter when you know what kind of investor you are and knowing that you are prone to make mistakes. As Oprah Winfrey said, "As you become more clear about who you really are, you'll be better able to decide what is best for you."

One way to help you remain true to yourself is to take a mental break from time to time. Every day you are bombarded with business news and investment tips with catchy headlines. Some of them are useful, but most are just noise shouted by the very opinionated anchors. Trying to catch every bit of information, every tip, is like running on an unstoppable treadmill. If you are searching for peace of mind, it is time to get off the treadmill by turning off Bloomberg and CNBC and just take a walk outside. This mental and physical break will give you time to think and reflect. As one of my favorite financial journalists, Jason Zweig, said, "The faster Wall Street runs, the more you should slow down and step back from that madness. Buy and hold an index fund forever, or study a few stocks with all the peace of mind you can muster."

Short-term detachment can be especially beneficial during a period of frustration, crisis, or chaos. It is very natural for us to react immediately. However, we often forget the simple truth that a person cannot see his or her own image in running water.

A savvy investor typically keeps his emotions in check. So don't check the performance of your portfolio every day, while checking your blood pressure only once a year. Some people like the excitement of the stock market, but for many, it is simply too much to handle. Checking your portfolio too frequently will likely lead you to make short-term emotional decisions, rather than long-term logical ones.

Knowing your own behavior bias doesn't mean to put yourself down. Don't forget that you are special. One can achieve neither the inner peace nor success if one lets self-doubt take control. So stop blaming yourself and stop forgetting your self-worth. Know who you are, what you are made of, and what values are important to you. Accept yourself as you are. Don't let self-doubt erode your confidence.

"At the center of your being
you have the answer;
you know who you are
and you know what you want."
— *Lao Tzu*

自知

Chinese for "understanding yourself"

Chapter 4
Maybe

Once upon a time there was an old farmer who had worked his crops for many years. One day his horse ran away. Upon hearing the news, his neighbors came to visit. "Such bad luck," they said sympathetically.

"Maybe," the farmer replied.

The next morning the horse returned, bringing with it three other wild horses. "How wonderful," the neighbors exclaimed.

"Maybe," replied the old man.

The following day, his son tried to ride one of the untamed horses, was thrown, and broke his leg. The neighbors again came to offer their sympathy on his misfortune.

"Maybe," answered the farmer.

The day after, military officials came to the village to draft young men into the army. Seeing that the son's leg was broken, they passed him by. The neighbors congratulated the farmer on how well things had turned out.

"Maybe," said the farmer.

The universe we live in is constantly changing. Nothing is static. Weakness can turn into strength and vice versa; it all depends on the situation. The only constant is change. The stock market moves like a pendulum. What's going up may come back down. Extended market exuberance is often followed by a correction—for example, markets reached record highs in October 2007 as investors rushed in, just prior to the most recent U.S. bear market. Investors become overconfident when the stock market rises and become overly fearful when the stock market goes down.

In 2011, I met a woman at a networking function. As soon as she learned that I am in the investment field, she told me that she sold all her investments in 2008. She believed cash was king. In early 2013, when I bumped into this woman again, she wanted to know what investments she should get back into because she heard the market had been up. Like a typical investor, she tried to time the market but failed. On the one hand, she cut her losses too soon in 2008. On the other hand, she waited too long to go back into the market and has missed out a great stock market recovery.

Let's face it, in the world of investing, there is only probability, no certainty. Most investors cannot time the market well because human nature works against most of us. Our natural instinct during periods of volatility is to stop the pain, not to endure it with patience. During a bear market, investors are scared by what they perceive as blood on the street, and most of the herd is selling. They tend to join the herd's panic sell. To buy during the market downturn means leaving the safety of the herd, standing out, risking humiliation. The pain of the loss lasts for a long time. When the market starts to recover, many retail investors choose to stay by the sideline and wait for certainty. By the time they finally join the crowd to buy again, they will end up investing at the top of the market.

As the classic comics character Pogo said, "We have met the enemy and he is us." If you let market activity flip-flop your thinking, you will forever be chasing what has already happened, instead of staying focused on what's next. Instead, acknowledge the fact that no one can predict the future movement of the stock market. Every day there is one expert predicting the next calamity is near, while another one warns you not to miss the next bull market.

The Charles Schwab Center for Financial Research looked at the 16 bear markets between 1926 and 2012 (markets with cumulative declines of greater than 10% and durations of at least six months) and found that in the first 12 months following the end of a bear market, a fully invested portfolio performed four times better than a portfolio that sat sidelined for six months before getting back into the market.

Warren Buffett once said, "Be fearful when others are greedy and be greedy only when others are fearful." As the world's greatest investor, he certainly understands the changing nature of the market and developed his own laser focus. Yet what Buffett is suggesting goes against every instinct we have. It requires a detached objectivity simply not possible when trading on emotion. That's why there is only one Warren Buffett.

But we humans love certainty and hate unexpected changes. When uncertainty sets in, we naturally want to follow the crowd. This is what "herd" mentality refers to. Psychologist Erich Fromm said that "The quest for certainty blocks the search for meaning. Uncertainty is the very condition to impel man to unfold his powers."

The word for "crisis" in Chinese contains two distinct meanings at the same time: danger and opportunity. Temporary setbacks are nature's way of giving us an opportunity to learn something from it. Zen masters recommend that we should welcome and respect changes enthusiastically, and take the unpredictable variations as opportunities to develop a stronger sense of self. If you don't like the current situation, give it enough time, it will change. Therefore, rather than worrying about short-term variations, we are better off focusing on our long-term goals and things that we have control over—our attitude and our behavior.

As Winston Churchill said, "Attitude is a little thing that makes a big difference." If you want to invest like a Zen master, keep your attitude toward change in check. Excessive craving for higher and higher returns will cost you dearly in the end. It could lead you to burnout or even lead you to self-destruction. Zen teaches us that "to be overjoyed at success and destroyed at failure is to become a victim of circumstances."

The shift between ups and downs is a market norm. Therefore, during a time of chaos, it is best to stay calm and not rush to react. Bill Gross, the former bond king from PIMCO who managed one of the largest bond funds in the world, mentioned during a Bloomberg interview that during the market turmoil, he often left his office and went to take a yoga class. All of us could achieve an inner peace by detaching ourselves from short-term outcomes, turning away from outside noises. If we ride out the difficult and discouraging times with a peaceful mindset, we will eventually achieve what we want. Zen believes that "The body with no tension and the mind with no intention are most adaptable to changes."

Paradoxically, when we let go of attachment to outcomes, success is often the result. Zen masters encourage us to achieve happiness through not being attached to the short-term outcomes. For investors, the following two-step approach will help them stay focused despite changes:

First, define your investment goal. You need to know what your investment goals are. Baseball hall-of-famer and noted philosopher Yogi Berra once said, "If you don't where you are going, you'll end up someplace else." This is never truer than when planning for your financial future. The first step in setting money goals is to identify what you want to achieve in the future. These goals may range from something decades in the future, like retirement, or months in the future, like a down payment on a home. Contributing to your children's college education? These are all considered to be money goals.

Many people's investment goal simply is to be rich. They mistakenly equate money with wealth. There are many people who make a lot of money but worry about things all the time, and they wait for the next paycheck or next bonus to finance an expensive car purchase or their kids' private schools. One of my friends labeled this group of people as "rich in W2, but poor in 1099." [1]

---

[1] W2 is a tax form that reports a person's wage income, while 1099 is another tax form that reports a person's other income such as interests, dividends, royalties, etc.

Money is a means to the end, but shouldn't be the end itself. What we really want to achieve is financial freedom. American writer Frank Herbert said, "Wealth is a tool of freedom, but the pursuit of wealth is the way to slavery." Pursuing wealth is a lifestyle choice that requires strong discipline and sustained effort.

We should take a leaf out of a pro golfer's book. Have you ever watched any top golfers compete? Good golfers' "mental toughness" comes from their undistracted and intense focus on the green (the ultimate long-term goal). When they occasionally hit the ball outside the fairway, they always walk a few steps back or walk sideways, while visualizing an optimal trajectory to the green in their mind. Therefore, their next shot will get them back to the green. Just like the golfers, we should not lose sight of our ultimate financial goal no matter what happens. It is true that sometimes things do happen which may cause us temporarily deviate from focusing on our financial goals. However, as soon as circumstances change, we should turn our focus back to our financial goal.

Second, once you clearly set your goals, you should create a plan to realize your goals. Too many investors have no investment plan at all—they merely react to the rumors and news of the market on the fly. If you fail to plan, then you are planning to fail. Research shows that investors who plan ahead experience better return. Your plan should identify which investment vehicle can best serve your desire to reach your goal, and at the same time, is suitable for your own risk tolerance and investment horizon. The beauty of having a written plan is that when some market events happen, or you hear some rumors and you have strong emotions to buy and sell, you can always go back to your written plan to help you fight off temptations and react to your emotions and events. You should only change your plan if your own needs or circumstances change.

As John F. Kennedy said, "Change is the law of life. And those who look only to the past or present are certain to miss the future." Embrace change!

應變

Chinese for "adjusting to change"

Chapter 5
It's All About Perspective

Whenever anyone asked him about Zen, the great master Gutei would quietly raise one finger into the air. A boy in the village began to imitate this behavior. Whenever he heard people talking about Gutei's teachings, he would interrupt the discussion and raise his finger. Gutei heard about the boy's mischief. When he saw him in the street, he seized him and bit his finger. The boy cried and began to run, but Gutei called out to him. When the boy turned to look, Gutei raised his finger into the air. At that moment the boy became enlightened.

It is human nature to compare ourselves to others and imitate their behaviors if we think they are more successful than we are. Often we think that we have to keep up with the Joneses because that's society's expectation. As Mark Twain described in his essay, *Corn Pone Opinions*, "The outside influences are always pouring in upon us, and we are always obeying their orders and accepting their verdicts!"

But we don't have to subscribe to either external pressure or our internal desperation to please if we understand perspective. We have all heard the saying that "The glass is half full" or "The glass is half empty." How about these: "The glass is twice as big as it needs to be." Or "The glass is full; half with water, half with air." Or "The water is surrounded by a glass." All these statements could be correct, depending perspectives.

Perspective is all about point of view. Our perspectives are often shaped by faith, culture, and experience. Abraham Lincoln said, "We can complain because rose bushes have thorns, or rejoice because thorn bushes have roses." Because our perspective will influence our actions and how we interact with others, we first need to recognize the limitation of our own perspective. We all have the tendency to search for information to confirm our existing beliefs, while avoiding contrary evidence. Psychologists call this behavior *confirmation bias*. You all probably heard the saying that "People who look through keyholes are apt to get the idea that most things are keyhole shaped." When we recognize the limitations of our own perspective, we learn to be humble.

Perspectives are often not the same as truth. Yet, applying different perspectives can be a life changing experience. I recently finished reading the biography of Steve Jobs by Walter Isaacson, and one incident in Job's childhood really struck me. As you may know, Jobs was adopted at birth. His birth mother was an unmarried grad student. The first couple who were going to adopt him changed their mind at the last minute because they wanted a girl. Eventually, he was adopted by a different couple, and when he was 6 or 7 years old, he found out about all of this. He was angry and ashamed. He felt abandoned and unwanted, and he confronted his adoptive parents and asked them why his birth parents didn't want him. His parents sat him down and said, "You are not abandoned. We specifically chose you." They said this slowly and repeated it several times to make sure young Steve understood. These compelling words didn't change nor deny the fact that he was adopted. However, these words changed his perspective on life. He was not abandoned. He was special and he was chosen. This perspective influenced him to accomplish all the great things he did later in life. "Sometimes when you're surrounded by dirt, you're a better witness for what's beautiful." (Matt de la Pena)

How does perspective influence investing? Your perspective of what investing is will influence how you invest, what you invest in, and your attitude and behavior toward investment gains and losses. If you think investing is no different from gambling, you will behave like a gambler. Investing will become a zero-sum game to you. You will have neither the patience nor the willingness to spend time on conducting analysis before making an investment. You are more likely to put your money into something because other people claim it to be a "good" investment. You probably won't stay in an investment very long; you may move in and out of your investment quickly, driven by rumors, rather than by understanding. Your decision-making process is more emotional than rational. If you made investment gains, you are going to credit it to good luck and your super stock-picking skill. If you lost money, you are likely to hold others responsible for your misfortune. You may become angry and frustrated. You may even resent other's investment success. To you, Wall Street is run by a group of fat cats who are out to exploit you and you just can't catch a break as an individual investor.

On the other hand, if you view each share of stock as a piece of ownership of an enterprise, you will behave like an owner. As Dr. Ben Carson has said, "When you stop making excuses, you start looking for solutions." Do you see any business owner get out of their business after only a few days? When you feel a sense of ownership, you will tend to choose your investments more carefully and once you invest, you tend to hold on to your investment longer. Yes, you care about your investment returns, but you probably also care about the people who run the business, and the product and service the business provides. In the past, I never liked to go to Lowe's, a home improvement store, because items such as paint brushes, plumbing supplies, and lumber seemed boring to me. Since I became a shareholder, however, each trip to Lowe's has become a joyful excursion. Paint brushes and lumber are just as interesting as shoes when I know that I own a small piece of it. I've also developed a great appreciation of how the store provides me with an abundance of choices so I can easily fix a problem or beautify my home.

It is worth pointing out that we Americans are very fortunate because we have the most developed market system in the world. Any one of us, can own a piece of any publicly traded American company, and many international corporations for as little as $7 a trade (commission) through an online discount broker. Not many people in the world have our kind of easy entrance to become a business owner.

The wonder of a free market economic system is its efficient allocation of capital. Rather than hiding money beneath your mattress, you can invest your capital with people and businesses that know how to maximize its return by providing the best product and services at the lowest cost. With an attitude and perspective of an owner, you just created a win-win situation.

Former U.S. Senator John Sununu said that "Perspective gives us the ability to accurately contrast the large with the small, and the important with the less important. Without it we are lost in a world where all ideas, news, and information look the same. We cannot differentiate, we cannot prioritize, and we cannot make good choices." So choose your perspective wisely and don't lose it when making investment decisions.

遠景

Chinese for "perspective"

Chapter 6
Cliffhanger

One day while walking through the wilderness a man stumbled upon a vicious tiger. He ran, but soon came to the edge of a high cliff. Desperate to save himself, he climbed down a vine and dangled over the fatal precipice. As he hung there, two mice appeared from a hole in the cliff and began gnawing on the vine.

Suddenly, he noticed on the vine a plump wild strawberry. He plucked it and popped it in his mouth. It was incredibly delicious!

I can never stop smiling whenever I read this story. The word for crisis in Chinese is actually a two-word phrase: 危机. 危 means *danger* and 机 means *opportunity*. Investing is, in essence, a process to determine one's risk and return trade-off. When you are willing to take certain amount of risk, you should receive a sweet reward in return.

What constitutes investment risk? Many average investors identify investment risk solely as the risk of losing investment principal. In fact, a typical investment, whether in stock or bonds, carries many different risks. All risks can be grouped into two categories: *systematic risks* and *unsystem-*

atic risks. Systematic risk, also known as "market risk" or "volatility," is the "uncertainty inherent to the entire market or entire market segment" (investopedia.com). All investments are subject to systematic risk (albeit in different severity) by factors like inflation, recession, and fluctuation of interest rates. Unsystematic risk, also known as "specific risk" or "diversifiable risk," is the type of risk that is unique to the company or industry you invest in. For example, if a CEO leaves his company unexpectedly, that is a specific risk to his company and its shareholders. Unsystematic risk can be reduced by investing in many different types of assets (aka diversification).

Since all investments come with risks, as an investor, you will not get a good investment return if you are not willing to take certain levels of risk. Yet a study released by Natixis Global Asset Management shows that investors aren't accepting the risk and return trade-offs. As a matter of fact, the study suggests 56% of investors want to achieve high returns but are only willing to take minimal risks. This phenomenon is often referred to as the "stock market avoidance." (Jaffe, 2014)

Many people don't realize the high cost of staying out of risky investments like stocks. According to a study done by Aswath Damodaran (you can find a link to this study in the "References" section), from 1928 to 2014, the annual return on stocks (measured by the S&P 500 index) was 11.53%, while the return on the 10-year Treasury bond was 5.28%. Based on his study, if you invested $100 in the S&P 500 index in 1928, you could expect to receive close to $290,000 in 2014. Conversely, if you invested your $100 in a 10-year Treasury bond over the same time period, you could expect to receive only around $7,000 in 2014. If you hold cash in U.S. dollars, your seemingly "safe" asset would have lost over 90% of its value due to inflation. If you don't care to go through his study, Table 1 is a hypothetical example to illustrate that over the long run, the stock market provides the best returns against other asset classes. So if growing your assets is your number-one priority, you have to be willing to take on some risks.

Table 1. Comparison of Investment Returns

Year/Asset Class	Growth Rate	$10,000 Becomes….
I. 20 Year Period		
Treasury Bills	4%	$21,911
Bonds	6%	$32,071
Average Mutual Funds	8%	$46,609
S&P 500	11%	$80,623
II. 60 Year Period		
Treasury Bills	4%	$105,196
Bonds	6%	$329,877
Average Mutual Funds	8%	$1,012,571
S&P 500	11%	$5,240,572

There is no doubt that investing in stocks generates better returns in the long run. So why do some investors shy away from stocks? Behavioral finance studies have found that investors are roughly twice as sensitive to losses as they are to gains. Have you ever noticed that many people on the street will not stop to pick up a dime, but they would certainly stop to pick up a dime if it fell out of their own pocket? Dan Ariely of the *Wall Street Journal* explained, "These might seem like the same case, but they aren't. When we pick up 10 cents, we add to our wealth, but when we reclaim a dime that we dropped, we prevent a loss- and preventing a loss is much more important and valuable." There is no doubt investors tend to evaluate gains and losses over a relatively short time horizon. This extreme fear of losses in the near term, combined with people's tendency to look at each investment in isolation, helps to explain low stock market participation rates.

After every big stock market drop, many investors tend to feel victimized. The truth is that it is normal for the stock market to go through cycles of booms, busts, ups, and pullbacks. So stop blaming others, and especially do not blame Wall Street. No one forces you into the stock market. You know there are risks associated with investing. Choose investments that fit your risk tolerance, not what's hot. A Chinese proverb summarizes this even better: *"He who blames others has a long way to go on his journey. He who blames himself is halfway there. He who blames no one has arrived."*

An interesting perspective about risk tolerance is how gender plays an important role. A study done by the BlackRock shows that women are generally more risk averse than men when it comes to saving and investing. The different attitude toward risks and investing between the different genders has even made it to pop culture.

I am a fan of the hit PBS show "Downton Abbey," a British drama series that follows the lives of the Crawley family and its servants from the late 19th century to the early 20th century. In episode 5 of season 5, Mrs. Patmore, the head cook from downstairs, just inherited 300 pounds from her deceased aunt. Now, 300 pounds may not sound like much today (around $450 at current exchange rates), but it was worth a lot more in 1924, the year in which season 5 was set. Mrs. Patmore is a prudent person, so she chose not to squander the money. But she didn't know what to do with it, so she asked the head butler, Mr. Carson, for financial advice. Why did she consult with Mr. Carson? She explained that Mr. Carson is a male and an authority figure to her.

It turned out Mr. Carson didn't know much about personal finance himself. But he was determined to maintain his authoritative status, so he suggested Mrs. Patmore purchase shares of a construction company with her inheritance. Mrs. Patmore was uncomfortable with this recommendation because she knew nothing about construction or investing in stocks. In the end, she purchased a cottage with her inheritance and started collecting rent.

You see, men and women respond to risk very differently and, therefore, make very different investment decisions. Men, generally, are more willing to make risky bets with their money. They often are thrill-seeking investors who tend to focus on the short-term track record of portfolio performance. Women, on the other hand, generally associate money with security. Therefore, women are typically very cautious and take their time to make investment decisions. Women often choose investments they feel they know something about and that also offers downside protection. This tendency often leads women to choose safer, but lower return, investments.

But women cannot afford to live with low return investments because women have longer life spans than men. *National Geograp*hic reported that in the U.S., women live longer—81 years on average, compared to 76 for men. Living longer means women need their money to last longer too. Therefore, women cannot afford to take little or no investment risks. Daniel Kahneman, a professor of psychology at Princeton, points out that "The real enemy of wealth accumulation is loss aversion.... In principle, if you have an individual who is trying to save for old age, the less sensitive they are emotionally to small fluctuations in their wealth, the better off they are going to do in the long run" (Nelson, 2012).

While I encourage you to take on some risks, I am not saying that you should put all your savings into the stock market. When I meet a new client, the first question I ask them is whether they have enough savings to cover 6-8 months' living expenses. If they do, this fund needs to remain in either a checking or a savings account, not in the stock market. Business goes through cycles. Every couple of years or decades, an economy will run into recession. The stock market will decline. If you put money that is supposed to cover your short-term needs into the stock market, you may be forced to sell it at a loss if you need the funds.

Investing is ultimately about the trade-off between risk and rewards. Often we have to overcome our own behavior bias in order to achieve the desired investment objectives. Fortunately, we do not have to do this in the dark. There are many online tools[2] that help us estimate the potential shortfalls based on our current investment choices. I highly recommend that you try them out. Keep in mind that they are not 100% accurate, but they can give you a rough idea of what the future may look like. If the calculation shows that you have a large shortfall, you may want to make some investment adjustments or seek help from a professional investment adviser.

---

[2] For example, www.bankrate.com offers a free calculator to help you estimate retirement income shortfall.

權衡

Chinese for "trade-off"

Chapter 7
The Fake Monk

A monk called himself the "Master of Silence." He was actually a fraud and had no genuine understanding. To sell his humbug Zen, he had two eloquent attendant monks to answer questions for him; but he himself never uttered a word, as if to show his inscrutable "silent Zen." One day, during the absence of his two attendants, a pilgrim monk came to him and asked: "Master, what is the Buddha?" Not knowing what to do or how to answer, in his confusion he could only look desperately around in all directions—east and west, here and there—for his missing mouthpieces.

But the pilgrim was very pleased and satisfied with this interview. He left the "Master" and set out again on his journey. On the road the pilgrim met the attendant monks on their way home, and began telling them enthusiastically what an enlightened being this "Master of Silence" was.

The pilgrim explained: "In answering my question as to what Zen was, he simply closed his eyes and said nothing. That was a clue to the famous saying: 'If one can close his eyes and sleep soundly in the deep recesses of the cloudy mountains he is a great monk indeed.' Oh, what an enlightened Zen master! How profound is his teaching!" The pilgrim continued his journey in a very high spirit because he believed he was enlightened by a true Zen master.

When the attendant monks returned to the temple where the "Master of Silence" is, the fake monk scolded them thus: "Where have you been all this time? A while ago I was embarrassed to death, and almost ruined, by an inquisitive pilgrim."

This story about the fake Zen master often reminded me of Bernie Madoff, who pulled off the most infamous Ponzi scheme in the 21st century. For many years before his scheme was exposed, he claimed to have the best investment record and he paid early investors unbelievably handsome investment returns, while in fact he used funds from new investors to pay investment returns to early investors as well as affording himself a luxurious lifestyle. Just like the fake Zen master in our story, Madoff kept a tight lip about his "winning" investment strategy. He kept a mystic atmosphere around him. His former title as the chairman of NASDAQ provided him a cover for his Ponzi scheme. To give the illusion that he was a highly sought-after expert, Madoff liked to drop names of SEC officials he knew and mentioned to others that he was on the "short list" to be the next SEC chairman. He even rejected some investors from time to time to maintain the façade of exclusivity of his service. Many investors have mistaken his job titles as a sign of talent, and they committed classic mistakes. As investors, there are a couple of lessons to be learned from the Madoff case:

1. Don't fall for the illusion that there is someone out there who can constantly beat the market, or there is some kind of investment that provides low risk and a consistent high return. Remember, we talked about the very definition of investing as a process of trade-off between risk and return. If you seek higher return, you have to be willing to take on more risk. There is no such thing as a low-risk, high-return investment. If anything sounds too good to be true, it is probably not true. Don't let your greed blind your judgment.

2. Greed is not a product of capitalism or the stock market. Greedy people have been around since our ancestors lived in caves. No matter which century we are in and no matter how much technological advancement we have, human nature won't change.

3. No one cares more about your money than you do. Don't outsource your judgment and due diligence to other people. Don't count on regulations from the SEC or FINRA catching all the bad guys. Regulators operate as if driving solely based on what they see from the rearview mirror. Remember when Madoff himself was surprised that he didn't get caught sooner by the SEC? Regulations only make the good guys' lives miserable. The bad guys can always find loopholes. Not everyone can or should be an investment expert; however, everyone should take some time to educate themselves to the extent that they can

to figure out who is a true financial expert and who is a fraud.

There are a little over 300,000 financial advisers in the U.S. Many are honest and hardworking people, who truly have their clients' best interests in mind. According to a study by the mutual fund giant Vanguard Group, a good financial adviser can add three percentage points to an investor's return. Good advisers are also good "behavior coaches" who can "act as emotional circuit breakers by circumventing clients' tendencies to chase returns or run for cover in emotionally charged markets." But how do you find a good adviser? After all, many financial professionals call themselves advisers, but they operate very differently. Not all investment/financial advisers are in the business of giving investment/financial advice. Here are some questions you should ask a potential adviser before you sign up with his or her service:

What credential do you have? Not all credentials are created equal. Some credentials have much more rigorous requirements than others. For example, the Chartered Financial Analyst (CFA) charter requires roughly 900 hours of study in accounting, economics, ethics, finance, and mathematics, after which students must pass three six-hour exams. On the other hand, a membership in the National Association of College Funding Advisors requires only 12 hours of study, only two hours of which is on financial aid and the rest of the time is devoted to marketing techniques. Therefore, it is important for you to find out not only what credential your potential advisers have, but also understand how difficult it is to get that credential.

How are you compensated? Advisers are generally compensated in three ways: *commission-only, fee-based,* and *fee-only*. Incentives influence behaviors. Remember the saying, "Never ask a barber if you need a haircut"? Commission-based advisers tend to be product-oriented or transaction-oriented because they have the financial incentive to sell. Fee-only advisers generally charge a percentage of assets under management or an hourly fee for financial advice/planning. Some of them are willing to negotiate a lower percentage if the assets under management reach a certain threshold, e.g., $500,000 or $1 million. Fee-based advisers' compensation is a combination of fees and commissions. Fee-only advisers disclose the percentage of fees or the hourly fee charged on the contract so clients know exactly how much the services cost, while commission-based advisers generally do not disclose their commission and are under no obligation to do so.

Who takes custody of the client's money? Some advisers offer investment services only, but do not take custody of clients' money. A third party, normally a brokerage firm, will take custody of the client's money and provide the adviser a platform to make investment decisions for the client. However, the same brokerage firm (aka custodian) will restrict any fund inflow and outflow by the advisers unless it has written authorization from the client. This restriction allows clients to have more control of their investments. At the same time, clients can withdraw funds directly with the custodian without advisers' intervention. In addition, clients can verify advisers' performance reports with separate statements from the custodian.

Not all advisers are organized in this way, though. Some advisers may have independent offices and business names, but they actually work for either a larger investment advisory firm or a brokerage firm. So the adviser's employer will take custody of clients' money. There is nothing wrong with this type of business model; it all depends on how much control the clients want.

What's your legal responsibility to your client? A registered investment adviser (RIA) is required by law to have a fiduciary duty to clients. Fiduciary comes from the Latin word *fiducia*, meaning "trust." The legal dictionary defines fiduciary as "An individual in whom another has placed the utmost trust and confidence to manage and protect property or money. The relationship wherein one person has an obligation to act for another's benefit."

Section 206 of the Investment Advisers Act of 1940 imposes a fiduciary duty on investment advisers by operation of law, which means investment advisers are legally bound to serve the best interests of their clients. However, many financial advisers and broker-dealers today are not subject to such a high ethical and legal standard. Instead, they are required only to ensure the investment recommendation is suitable for clients and they provide clients with the best execution of trades.[3]

---

[3] On February 23, 2015, President Obama called for tougher standards on brokers who manage retirement savings accounts. As a result, the

Be careful who you consult for investment advice. Many people who exude a presence of authority and probably are brilliant in their own professional fields don't know much about investing. Since most people are not comfortable with managing investments on their own, it is important to consult with the right expert for advice. As the saying goes, "Not everything that shines is gold." The Wizard of Oz turned out to be a fraud. So asking the right questions will help you find the right expert.

Department of Labor is working on a proposal that will subject brokers to more scrutiny.

信任

Chinese for "trust"

Chapter 8
Can You Make an Egg Stand?

In 1418, a competition was announced in Florence, Italy. The city's magnificent cathedral, Santa Maria del Fiore, had been under construction for more than a hundred years by then. Its original design called for a grand dome to be built. The dome was supposed be an octagonal shape, higher and wider than any that had ever been built, with no external buttresses to keep it from spreading and falling under its own weight. For over a century, no one knew how to build it.

Opera del Duomo—the office in charge of the cathedral, asked artisans, carpenters, and masons from all over Italy to submit proposals for the grand dome. After very careful evaluation, Filippo Brunelleschi's design proposal was by far the best. Yet he was a trained goldsmith, not a known architect. The Opera was concerned about granting such a significant project to an unknown architect, so they asked Brunelleschi to give a detailed explanation of his proposal. Brunelleschi suggested to the members of the Opera that whoever could make an egg stand on a flat piece of marble should win the commission. When all the other contestants failed the test, Filippo simply cracked the egg on the bottom and then stood it upright. When his rivals protested that they might have done the same, Filippo retorted that they would know how to build the dome too, if only they knew his plan. So the commission to build the dome went to Brunelleschi.

Brunelleschi's solutions were ingenious. To build this grand dome without external buttresses, he created an architectural illusion by building a double shell of the dome. He embedded iron chains within the inner dome to keep the dome from spreading and falling under its weight. It took 14 years to construct the dome, which is comprised of over four million bricks. When it was completed, the dome was 375 feet high (a 30-story building is about 300 feet high) and 144 feet wide. It is higher and wider than any brick and motor dome that has ever been built. To put it into perspective, Michelangelo's dome of St. Peter's is almost 10 feet narrower. The dome of the Capitol in Washington, D.C., is less than two-thirds the size of Brunelleschi's dome.

This story is obviously is not from Zen's teaching, but it has the kind of quality of a Zen story. I was able to visit Brunelleschi's dome in Florence and it is truly a remarkable building. Brunelleschi was able to build this architectural masterpiece because he was able to come up with a genius, yet at the same time incredibly simple, solution.

Today, we live in an increasingly complex world. It seems that no solution is a good solution unless it is a complicated one. It seems no law is a good law unless it is written in hundreds and thousands of pages. It seems that we cannot get anything done unless we spend hours in meetings. Nancy Koehn, a professor from the Harvard Business School, estimates that there will be 11 million meetings taking place just today. The truth is, simplicity is much more difficult to achieve than complexity.

Simplicity has great implications in investment portfolio construction. In the early chapters, we discussed the importance of diversification in your investment portfolio, meaning you can reduce unsystematic risk of your portfolio if you invest in a variety of asset classes, sectors, or even geographic locations. But many investors mistakenly think it means that the more different types of investments in a portfolio, the lower the risk. This notion couldn't be further from the truth. It is important to keep in mind two things about diversification and risk: first, no matter how diversified you are, you will never eliminate all risks; second, there is an optimal point that, once reached, adding additional assets won't further reduce any risks, but on the contrary, could very likely increase risks.

In Edwin J. Elton and Martin J. Gruber's book, *Modern Portfolio Theory and Investment Analysis*, they conclude that an all-equity portfolio is close to achieving optimal diversification with 20 stocks. Therefore, many average investors can reduce risks and trading costs through a simple portfolio consisting of a few broad index-based mutual funds and exchange-traded funds (ETFs).

Yes, investing in index funds can be a boring experience. Yet this approach can yield many benefits, including saving transaction costs, management fees, etc. Most importantly, it will enable you to stop worrying about things you can't control. When you stop worrying, you can focus your time and energy on what makes you happy. That is truly what wealth is about. Wealth is freedom. It is to free you from worrying so you can make your own choices to pursue what makes you happy. Wealth will turn a person from being a slave of the debt to a master of his own destiny.

In 2014, Warren Buffett talked about his investment plan for his wife after his passing: "My advice to the trustee could not be more simple: Put 10% of the cash in short-term government bonds and 90% in a very low-cost S&P 500 index fund. (I suggest Vanguard's.) I believe the trust's long-term results from this policy will be superior to those attained by most investors—whether pension funds, institutions, or individuals—who employ high-fee managers." In essence, the world's greatest investor will create an investment portfolio with only two funds for his own loved one; you can't get simpler than this.

For most investors who have moderate return requirements and low risk tolerance, choosing a few well-diversified index funds has worked wonders through the years. Statistical evidence shows many investors, including professionals, likely underperform against the S&P 500. Instead of chasing exotic investment ideas, many ordinary investors will be better off buying and holding low cost and well-diversified index funds.

As another great Renaissance artist, Leonardo da Vinci, stated, "Simplicity is the ultimate sophistication."

If you ask an investor why he invests, a likely answer is to preserve and grow wealth. But what is wealth? Wealth is not measured by a dollar figure. There are plenty of millionaires and billionaires who still do not feel wealthy. Wealth is freedom. It frees you from worrying so you can make your own choices to pursue what makes you happy. Wealth will turn a person from being a slave of the debt to a master of his own destiny. Once you understand what wealth truly is, how to reach wealth becomes incredibly simple and straightforward. First, don't spend more than you earn. Second, invest your savings in a simple but well-diversified portfolio and hold on to it for a long time.

簡單

Chinese for "simplicity"

Conclusion

How Long Does it Take to Become a Master?

A martial arts student went to his teacher and said earnestly, "I am devoted to studying your martial system. How long will it take me to master it."

The teacher's reply was casual: "Ten years." Impatiently, the student answered, "But I want to master it faster than that. I will work very hard. I will practice every day, ten or more hours a day if I have to. How long will it take then?"

The teacher thought for a moment. "20 years."

Many of us are very impatient, especially when we have instant access to a vast amount of information at our fingertips. Just like the martial arts student, any amount of waiting seems too long. We want instant gratification; we want to be good at something swiftly; most of all, we want to get rich fast. Many of us get in and out of an investment hastily, searching for the best investment to build wealth quickly. But as Benjamin Graham wrote in his book *The Intelligent Investor,* "There are no sure and easy paths to riches on Wall Street or anywhere else." As a matter of fact, the wisdom of

Zen masters teaches us that there is no shortcut to any place that is worth going. Often, like the hare that lost the race against the turtle, what prevents us from achieving our goals is our own behavior. You see, the wisdom of the Zen master is to show us that the greatest wisdom is often the plain truth that stands right in front of us.

The timeless stories and philosophy from ancient Zen masters teach us that building long last wealth doesn't require us to have complex strategies. A simple investment plan will work beautifully if we learn to avoid common behavior mistakes and learn to become an investor who is:

- **Adaptable**—embraces change enthusiastically
- **Disciplined**—knows how to fight off temptations and remain focused
- **Honest**—ready to admit past mistakes
- **Humble**—doesn't presume to have all the answers
- **Patient**— willing to delay gratification
- **Behaving like a business owner**—willing to invest in other's success
- **A lifelong student**— acknowledges the unknown and always sets aside time for quiet thinking and reading

Investing like a Zen master is not a passive experience; rather, you are empowered and engaged in a different way. If you can learn from the Zen masters, you can achieve financial security and inner peace, and live happily ever after.

References

Ariely, D. (2015). Retrieved from: http://online.wsj.com/search/term.html?KEYWORDS=Dan+Ariely&mod=DNH_S

Ayres, I., Ayton, P., Davies, G. B., Fasolo, B., Hens, T., Iyenger, S., Koh, A., Stewart, N., Sutherland, R., and Xia, C. (2011). "Risk and Rules: The Role of Control in Financial Decision Making," Barclays Wealth Insights, vol. 13.

Damodaran, A. (2015). *Annual Returns on Stock, T.Bonds and T.Bills: 1928 – Current.* Retrieved from: http://pages.stern.nyu.edu/~adamodar/New_Home_Page/datafile/histretSP.html

Jaffe, C. (2014). *Proof most investors are clueless.* Retrieved from: http://www.marketwatch.com/story/proof-most-investors-are-clueless-2014-05-12

King, R. (2013). *Brunelleschi's Dome: How a Renaissance Genius Reinvented Architecture*, Bloomsbury, USA.

Kuhnhenn, J. (2015). *Obama seeks tougher rules on retirement investment advisors.* Retrieved from: http://www.mercurynews.com/business/ci_27584173/obama-seeks-tougher-rules-retirement-investment-advisors

The Marshmallow Test. (2009). IgniterMedia. Retrieved from: htttps://www.youtube.com/watch?v=QX_oy9614HQ

Mischel, W. (2014). *The Marshmallow Test*, Little Brown and Company.

Murray, N. (2000). *Simple Wealth, Inevitable Wealth.*

Nelson, C. (2012, October). *Journal of Financial Planning.*

Oster, N. (2015). *Men vs. Women: Risk Aversion.* Retrieved from: http://www.blackrockblog.com/2013/11/06/men-women-risk-aversion/

Osterland, A. (2014). *Advisors slow to train successors.* Retrieved from: http://www.cnbc.com/id/101621040

Sehgal, K. (2015). *This is Your Brian on Money.* Retrieved from: http://www.marketwatch.com/story/this-is-your-brain-on-money-2015-03-10?dist=lcountdown

Shefrin, H. (2007). *Beyond Greed and Fear: Understanding Behavioral Finance and the Psychology of Investing.*

Skinner, L. (2014). *Advisers can add 3 percentage points to clients' net returns. Retrieved from:* http://www.investmentnews.com/staff/lskinner

Svenson, O. (1981). *Are we less risky and more skillful than our fellow drivers?* Acta Psychologica, 47, 143-151.

Ten Short Zen Stories. Retrieved from: http://theunboundedspirit.com/10-short-zen-stories/

Thum, M. *10 Best Zen Stories.* Retrieved from: http://www.scribd.com/doc/99103803/The-10-Very-Best-Zen-Stories-Myrko-Thum#scribd

"U.S. Life Expectancy Map: The Gender Gap," *National Geographic*, retrieved from: http://news.nationalgeographic.com/news/2013/04/life-expectancy-map/

Woodley, K. (2014). *Why Warren Buffett Suggests Vanguard Funds.* Retrieved from: http://investorplace.com/2014/06/warren-buffett-vanguard-funds/#.VPTQinzF_JY

Zweig, J. (2014). *Giving Yourself an Investing Makeover,* the Wall Street Journal. Retrieved from: http://blogs.wsj.com/moneybeat/2014/05/23/giving-yourself-an-investing-makeover/

About the Author

Helen Raleigh, an immigrant from China who is fluent in both English and Chinese, is the owner of Red Meadow Advisors, LLC, a Colorado-based fee-only investment advisory firm. She has over 15 years' experience in the financial services industry in areas ranging from pension funds to risk management. She holds the "gold standard" investment industry certification—the Chartered Financial Analyst (CFA) charter—and Project Management Professional (PMP) certification. She recently served on the advisory board of the Business for Responsible Government Group at the South Metro Denver Chamber of Commerce, as well as the board of CFA Society Colorado. In addition to running her own investment advisory practice, Helen published her first book, *Confucius Never Said*, which was the 2015 silver winner of the Benjamin Franklin Award by the Independent Book Publishers Association (IBPA). You can also find her writings in various other publications, including the *Wall Street Journal*, the *Denver Post*, *CFA Institute Magazine*, and other media outlets.

    Helen earned her master's degree in business economics from the State University of New York, College of Oneonta, as well as a master's degree in business administration from the University of Wyoming.

www.ingramcontent.com/pod-product-compliance
Lightning Source LLC
Chambersburg PA
CBHW021018180526
45163CB00005B/2002